T0068771

THE BRONTË STORY

Some people have a special talent, for music, or for drawing and painting, or for writing. No one knows where this talent comes from. Perhaps people are born with it; perhaps it comes from God. Or perhaps it is chance or luck that allows this talent to grow, like sunshine bringing a plant into flower.

The special talent of three of the Brontë girls was for writing. No one taught them to write – they taught themselves, and the three of them wrote some of the great novels of the nineteenth century. But life was not easy at home in Haworth. The family was not rich, and the children had to work for a living. And one by one, illness and death cut off their lives and their talents. But the novels written by Charlotte, Emily, and Anne live on, year after year.

This is not one of the stories they wrote; it is about them. It is the story that their father did not write, but might have written: the story of the family that he had for such a short time.

OXFORD BOOKWORMS LIBRARY

True Stories

The Brontë Story

Stage 3 (1000 headwords)

Series Editor: Jennifer Bassett
Founder Editor: Tricia Hedge
Activities Editors: Jennifer Bassett and Alison Baxter

TIM VICARY

The Brontë Story

OXFORD UNIVERSITY PRESS

OXFORD
UNIVERSITY PRESS

Great Clarendon Street, Oxford OX2 6DP

Oxford University Press is a department of the University of Oxford.
It furthers the University's objective of excellence in research, scholarship,
and education by publishing worldwide in

Oxford New York

Auckland Cape Town Dar es Salaam Hong Kong Karachi
Kuala Lumpur Madrid Melbourne Mexico City Nairobi
New Delhi Shanghai Taipei Toronto

With offices in

Argentina Austria Brazil Chile Czech Republic France Greece
Guatemala Hungary Italy Japan Poland Portugal Singapore
South Korea Switzerland Thailand Turkey Ukraine Vietnam

OXFORD and OXFORD ENGLISH are registered trade marks of
Oxford University Press in the UK and in certain other countries

This edition © Oxford University Press 2008

The moral rights of the author have been asserted

Database right Oxford University Press (maker)

First published in Oxford Bookworms 1991

10 9

No unauthorized photocopying

All rights reserved. No part of this publication may be reproduced,
stored in a retrieval system, or transmitted, in any form or by any means,
without the prior permission in writing of Oxford University Press,
or as expressly permitted by law, or under terms agreed with the appropriate
reprographics rights organization. Enquiries concerning reproduction
outside the scope of the above should be sent to the ELT Rights Department,
Oxford University Press, at the address above

You must not circulate this book in any other binding or cover
and you must impose this same condition on any acquirer

Any websites referred to in this publication are in the public domain and
their addresses are provided by Oxford University Press for information only.
Oxford University Press disclaims any responsibility for the content

ISBN 978 0 19 479109 0

Printed in China

*The publishers would like to thank the following
for their permission to reproduce photographs:*
The Brontë Society (at the Brontë Parsonage Museum, Haworth),
and the National Portrait Gallery, London (pages 45, 52)

We would also like to thank Kathryn White of the Brontë Society
for her valuable help with the photographs

Word count (main text): 10,600 words

For more information on the Oxford Bookworms Library,
visit www.oup.com/elt/bookworms

CONTENTS

Haworth

There was a cold wind this afternoon, but the sun shone for an hour or two. I walked out on the moors behind the house. The sheep were hiding from the wind under the stone walls, and there were grey clouds over the hills to the west. It is only November, but I could smell snow in the air.

It will be a cold winter, this year of 1855.

My name is Patrick Brontë, and I am seventy-eight years old. I am the rector of the village of Haworth. Haworth is a village of small, grey stone houses on the side of a hill in the north of England, and I live in a house at the top of the hill, next to the church and the graveyard.

I walked through the graveyard to the church this afternoon.

The house at Haworth
'I live in a house next to the church and the graveyard.'

All my family except Anne are buried there. The wind had blown some dead leaves through the door into the church, and I watched them dancing in the sunlight near the grave. Soon I shall be in that grave with my wife and children, under the cold grey stone and dancing leaves.

It is dark outside now, and it is very quiet in this house. Charlotte's husband, Mr Nicholls, is reading in his room, and our servant is cooking in the kitchen. Only the three of us live here now. It is very quiet. I can hear the sounds of the wood burning in the fire, and the big clock on the stairs.

There is another sound too – the sound of the wind outside. The wind has many voices. It sings and laughs and shouts to itself all night long. Last night it cried like a little child, and I got out of bed and went to the window to listen.

There was no child, of course. Only the wind and the gravestones, cold in the pale moonlight. But I decided then that I would write the story of my children, today, before it is too late. Charlotte's friend, Mrs Gaskell, is writing a book about her, and perhaps she will want to read my story.

It is a fine story. It began in April 1820, when we came to Haworth for the first time . . .

There was a strong wind blowing that day too, out of a dark, cloudy sky. We could see snow on the moors. The road to Haworth goes up a hill, and there was ice on the stones of the road. Maria, my wife, was afraid to ride up the hill in the carts.

'We'll walk, children,' she said. 'If one of those horses falls down, there'll be a terrible accident. Come on, let's go and see our new house.'

Patrick Brontë
'I was the new rector for the village of Haworth.'

She was a small woman, my wife, and not very strong. But she carried the baby, Anne, up the hill in her arms. I carried Emily – she was one and a half years old then. The others walked. My two-year-old son, Patrick Branwell, walked with me, and Charlotte, who was nearly four, walked with her mother. The two oldest children – Elizabeth and Maria – ran on in front. They

Mrs Maria Brontë
'She was a small woman, my wife, and not very strong.'

were very excited, and laughed and talked all the way.

The people of Haworth came out to watch us. Some of them helped, but most of them just stood in their doorways and watched. They are very poor people, in this village. I was their new rector.

We had seven carts to carry our furniture up that icy hill, but it was hard work for the horses. When we reached our house, the wind was blowing hard in our faces. My wife hurried inside, and began to light fires.

'Do you like it, my dear?' I asked her that night, when the children were in bed. She looked pale and tired. I thought it was because of the long journey, and the children. Perhaps it was.

She held out her hands to the fire, and said: 'Of course, Patrick. It's a fine house. I do hope it will be a good home for you, and the children.'

I was a little surprised by that. 'And for you, Maria,' I said. 'Don't forget yourself. You are the most important person in the world, to me.'

She smiled then – a lovely smile. 'Thank you, Patrick,' she said. She was a very small woman, and she was often tired because of the children. But when she smiled at me like that, I thought she was the most beautiful woman in England.

A year and a half later, she was dead.

She did not die quickly. She was in bed for seven long months, in awful pain. The doctor came often, and her sister Elizabeth came too, to help. The children were ill, as well. It was a terrible time.

My wife Maria died in September, 1821. She was thirty-eight. It was my job to bury her in the church. Our six young children stood and watched quietly.

Afterwards, we went back to the house. I called them into this room and spoke to them.

I said: 'You must not cry too much, my dears. Your mother is with God now. She is happy. One day you will all die, and if you are good, you will go to God too.'

'But why?' Maria asked. 'Why did she die now, father? We need her.'

'This world is a hard place, children, and we cannot understand everything that God does. But God loves us, never forget that. Your mother loved you, and perhaps she can see you now. We must all try to work hard, learn as much as possible, and be kind to each other. Will you do that?'

'Yes, father.'

They all looked so sad, I remember, and they listened so carefully. Little Emily said: 'Who will be our mother now?'

'Maria is the oldest, so she will help me. You must all listen to her, and do what she says. And your Aunt Elizabeth is here, too. Perhaps she will stay for a while.'

Elizabeth did stay. She was older than my wife, and she wasn't married. We called her Aunt Branwell. She came from Penzance in Cornwall, a warm, sunny place by the sea in the south-west of England. It is often cold on the moors behind Haworth, and the winds blow all winter. Aunt Branwell hated Haworth, but she stayed here all her life, to help me with her sister's children. She was a good, kind woman.

I was very proud of my little Maria. She was only eight years old, but she worked all day like an adult. She helped the little

ones to get washed and dressed; she helped them to play and draw and read. She was like a little mother to them.

She could read very well herself. We always had books and newspapers in the house, and I talked to the children about them every day. I talked to them about adult things: the Duke of Wellington, and the important things that he was doing in

Elizabeth Branwell, Maria Brontë's sister
'Aunt Branwell was a good, kind woman.'

London. The children listened carefully, and tried hard to understand. Maria often read to the others from the newspaper, and asked me questions about it. She understood it better than most men.

I was sure my children were very clever. But I did not have time to talk to them all day; I had my work to do. So, in 1824, I sent them to school.

Cowan Bridge School

I was born in a small house in Ireland. There were only two rooms in our house, and I had nine brothers and sisters. My parents were very poor. We had no money, and only a small farm. But we did have a church near us, and that church had a school.

That school gave me my one chance of success. I worked very hard there, and when I was sixteen, I became a teacher. Then I went to St John's College, Cambridge, to study some more. I became a curate. When I married, I was able to get a good job and a house for my family. I got all that because I worked so hard at school.

I wanted my children to go to the best school that I could find. Cowan Bridge School was a school for the daughters of

The house where Patrick Brontë was born
'I was born in a small house in Ireland. It had only two rooms.'

churchmen. It belonged to a churchman – Mr Wilson. He was a good man, I thought. I liked the school, and it was not too expensive. So, in July 1824, I took Maria and Elizabeth there. In September, I took Charlotte and, in November, Emily as well. Emily was just six then, and Charlotte was eight.

I remember how quiet the house was that autumn. In the evenings I taught my son, Branwell, and my wife's sister looked after the youngest child, Anne. I often thought about the girls. My eldest, Maria, was a good, clever girl – I thought she must be the best pupil in the school. I waited for her letters, and wondered what new things she was learning.

She did tell me some things in her letters, but not enough. She told me she liked the schoolwork, and I was pleased. But she did not tell me about the food, or the cold, or the unkind teachers. Charlotte told me those things, much later. I know Maria did not tell me that the food was often burnt and uneatable, or that they could not sleep because the beds were too cold. She did not tell me that the poor hungry children had to wash with ice in the morning, and walk through wet snow to sit for two hours with icy feet in a cold church on Sundays. She did not tell me that many of the children at the school were ill.

You didn't tell me that, did you, Maria? Did you? Or did you try to write something, and stop because you were afraid of the teachers? You were a good, brave child, and I was so proud of you, so pleased because you were at school. I wanted you to learn everything; I didn't want you to be poor like my sisters. God help me, I thought you were happy at Cowan Bridge School!

Cowan Bridge School
*'Maria did not tell me about the food, or the cold, or
the unkind teachers.'*

There were no Christmas holidays at the school, and it was too difficult to travel over the cold, windy hills to visit my little girls. So I sat at home here in Haworth, with Aunt Branwell, my son, and the little girl, Anne. Outside, the wind blew snow over the gravestones, and there was ice on our windows.

On Christmas Day little Anne looked lonely. She asked me about her sisters.

'Don't worry, my dear,' I said. 'They are happy, with the other girls at school. You shall go to Cowan Bridge, too, when you are older.'

I remember how strangely she looked at me then. She was only four, and very pretty. She smiled at me, but her face went very white, and her hands started to shake. I don't know why. I thought she was cold, and I put some more wood on the fire. Then Aunt Branwell read her a story from the Bible, and I forgot about it.

In February a letter came. It was in an adult's handwriting, not Maria's. *Dear Mr Brontë*, it said. *I am afraid I have some bad news for you. Many children in the school have been ill, and your daughter Maria . . .*

My hand began to shake badly, and I dropped the letter on the floor. As I picked it up, I could see only one word – *dead . . . If your daughter Maria does not come home soon, she will be dead.*

I went over the hills to bring her back. My Maria was in a small bed in a cold room upstairs, coughing badly. Elizabeth and Charlotte and Emily stood beside her, waiting for me. They looked so sad and ill and frightened. I remember the big eyes in their small white faces. But I did not bring them home then; the school doctor said it was not necessary. So I took Maria home across the cold, windy moors to Haworth. I sat beside her in the coach and held her hand all the way. I remember how cold her hand was in mine. Thin cold fingers, that did not move at all.

It was too late to save her. She lay in bed upstairs for nearly three months, but she was too ill to eat. Her poor face was white, I remember, and it seemed thin and small like a dead child's. Only her eyes looked alive – big dark eyes in a thin white face. 'Don't cry, father,' she said to me once. 'I shall be with mother soon, you know. And with God.'

I buried Maria beside her mother, and a month later I buried Elizabeth there, too. She became ill at school, and a woman from the school brought her home. I brought Charlotte and Emily home two weeks later. They were here when Elizabeth

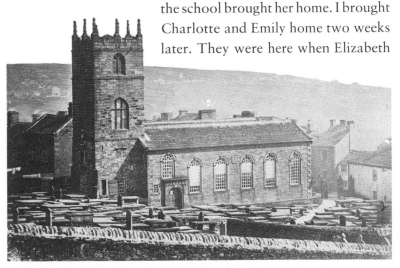

Haworth Church
'I buried Maria and Elizabeth beside their mother in the church.'

died. Her body lay all night in a wooden box on the table, and her little sisters and brother kissed her before she was buried.

I had wanted so much for these two girls, and now I had nothing. I stood in the church, and looked at the summer flowers I had put on their grave. I remembered how my wife had held the girls in her arms, and how she had smiled at me when we looked at them. 'They have come back to you now, Maria,' I said. 'I am sorry. I am so sorry, my love.'

The little books

I had four children now – Charlotte, Branwell, Emily and Anne. I did not send them to school again for many years. God's ways are hard to understand, I thought. Perhaps God was not pleased with me; perhaps He wanted Maria and Elizabeth for Himself. I decided to keep the others at home. Aunt Branwell could teach them, and I could help when I had time.

They were clever children, quick at learning. They loved to write and draw and paint, and they talked all day long. And, thank God, they were not ill. In the afternoons, my servant, Tabby, took them for long walks on the moors behind the house. They walked for miles on the hilltops in the strong clean wind, alone with the birds and the sheep. I think it was good for them.

They grew stronger, and there was a bright light in their eyes.

I was not the only sad father in Haworth. Many, many children died, and I had to bury them all. The water in Haworth was bad, so many children died from illness. And many more died from accidents; I saw a hundred children die from fire. In

Haworth village (in the early 1900s)
'Many children in Haworth died, and I had to bury them all.'

my house, I was always very careful. I had no curtains, no carpets, because I was afraid of fire. My children never wore cotton clothes, because they burn so easily.

One day in 1826 I brought a box of toy soldiers home from Leeds. Next morning the children began to play games with them.

'This one is mine!' Charlotte said. 'He's the Duke of Wellington!'

'And this is mine!' said Branwell. 'He's Napoleon Bonaparte!'

The children liked the wooden soldiers and began to tell a story about them. It was a very exciting story, I remember. They read it to me and Aunt Branwell and Tabby, our servant. The next day they invented another story, and then another. And then for several days the children were very quiet, and I wondered what they were doing.

I went upstairs, and opened their bedroom door. Inside, they were all busily writing or drawing on small pieces of paper. The wooden soldiers were in the middle of the room in front of them.

'What are you doing?' I asked.

Emily looked up. 'Oh, father, please go away,' she said. 'We're writing our secret books.'

I suppose I looked sad. 'What? Can't I see them?' I asked.

They all thought for a minute. Then Charlotte said, very seriously: 'You can see some of them, of course, papa. But they aren't easy to read, because it's very small writing. We'll show them to you when we are ready.'

These toy soldiers opened a new world for my children. They showed me some of their stories, but there were hundreds that they kept secret. They all began writing so young – Charlotte, the oldest, was only ten, and Emily was eight. I don't think they ever stopped. Mr Nicholls has all Charlotte's little books now, in a cupboard in his room. Some of them are no more than five or six centimetres high. They are beautifully made, and full of small pictures and tiny writing. There is one on my desk now, but I can't read it, my eyes are too bad.

Charlotte and Branwell wrote about a country called Angria, while Emily and Anne wrote about a land called Gondal. The people in those countries fought battles and fell in love, and

The little books
'They are beautifully made, and full of tiny writing.'

wrote letters and poems. My children wrote these poems and letters, and they wrote books about Angria and Gondal. They drew maps of the countries, wrote newspapers about them, and drew pictures of the towns and people in their stories. They invented a new world for themselves.

They wrote many of these stories when I was in bed. I used to read to the family, and pray with them in the evening, and then I usually went to bed at nine o'clock. One night, I remember, I woke up and came down again at ten. There was a noise in my room – this room where I am writing now. I opened the door and saw Charlotte and Branwell with a candle, looking at a picture on my wall.

'What are you doing here?' I asked.

'We're looking at the picture, papa,' Branwell said. 'It's the Duke of Zamorna and the Duke of Northangerland fighting in Glasstown.'

I looked at the picture. It's here now behind me. It's a picture of a story in the Bible, with a town, mountains, and hundreds of people in it. 'What do you mean?' I asked.

'It's one of our stories, papa,' Charlotte said. 'We have to come in here to look at the picture. Then we invent what happens.'

'Tell me, then,' I said. They both looked very excited; their faces were pink, and their eyes were bright in the candlelight. But they looked happy too. I put my candle on the table, and sat down here, where I am sitting now, to listen to their story.

It was a wonderful story. Charlotte's wooden soldier, the Duke of Wellington, had had a son, Arthur, Duke of Zamorna. Branwell's toy soldier, Bonaparte, had become the strong, bad, good-looking Duke of Northangerland. The two Dukes were fighting a terrible battle in a city called Glasstown. There were soldiers who died bravely, and beautiful women who fell in love. I listened until two o'clock in the morning. There was much more, but I have forgotten it now.

But I remember the excitement in my children's faces. Sometimes I thought they could actually see these people, as they talked.

Next day they said no more about it, and I did not ask. It was their own secret world, and they did not let me into it again. But I was pleased they had told me about it once. And sometimes they showed me drawings of places in Angria or Gondal. All my children could draw and paint beautifully. Charlotte used water-colours, and often spent hours painting small pictures. Branwell used oil-paints as well.

Anne Brontë's dog, Flossy, drawn by Charlotte
'All my children could draw and paint beautifully,'

4

Growing up

When Branwell was fourteen or fifteen, he did a lot of oil-paintings. He painted people in the village, and it was easy to recognize the faces in the pictures. Later, he did a fine painting of his three sisters. I was very proud of him. We all decided he would become a famous artist.

Charlotte went to school again when she was fifteen. It was a much better school – Miss Wooler's school at Roe Head. I don't think Charlotte liked school, but she wanted to be a teacher – a governess – so she worked hard. I taught Branwell at home, and Aunt Branwell taught Emily and Anne. The girls and Branwell were learning to play the piano, and Branwell played the music in church.

Emily and Anne had dogs, and they used to take them for walks on the moors. Anne's dog was called Flossy, and Emily had a big strong one called Keeper. Keeper went everywhere with her – I think Emily loved that dog more than any person. Emily was sometimes a difficult child. She was very shy, and did not

Patrick Brontë's study
'The girls and Branwell were learning to play the piano.'

often speak to anyone outside the family. When she was older, I sent her to school with Charlotte, but she hated it, so I brought her home and sent Anne instead.

Branwell was not shy. He could talk to anyone for hours. Everyone in Haworth liked him. I remember the day in 1835 when Branwell went to London. He was eighteen years old, and he was going to the Royal Academy in London to learn to be an artist. He walked down the hill in Haworth with a bag of his best paintings on his back, and everyone in the village came out to see him go. That was a great day for me.

Something terrible happened in London, but I don't know what it was. Branwell came back two weeks later, his face white, his clothes dirty. I don't know where he went or what happened in London. He refused to tell me. He just sat upstairs, alone in his room for hours.

Later, I paid for a room in Bradford for him to work in. He could paint pictures of famous people there, I thought. It was easy work for him. But he couldn't do it. He spent all my money, and came home again after a while.

This was a sad time for me. My eyes were very bad, and I had to pay a young curate to help me with my work for the church. My old servant, Tabby, broke her leg and was very ill. And then one day I got a letter from Miss Wooler's school. My curate read it to me.

Dear Mr Brontë, the letter said. *I am afraid that your daughter Anne is very ill, and . . .*

I don't think I ever moved so fast in all my life. Six hours later, I was at Roe Head. The next day Anne and Charlotte were home.

Anne was still alive, thank God! A month later she was well again. *Thank God.*

Miss Wooler's school at Roe Head, drawn by Anne Brontë
'One day I got a letter from Miss Wooler's school ...'

All my children were safe at home.

I was happy to have them here. They were so clever, and kind, and they loved each other so much. But I was an old man with bad eyes, and Aunt Branwell and I had very little money. My children had to find work somewhere, in order to live.

But what sort of work could they do?

5

Looking for work

I do not remember everything they did. Charlotte and Anne worked as governesses for some months, teaching rich children in big houses, and Branwell got a job like that too, for a while. But they didn't like their work. At home my children were full of talk and laughter, but away from home they were shy, quiet, unhappy.

They wrote a lot of letters in their search for work – sometimes to famous people. Branwell wanted to be a writer, so he wrote to writers; but not many of them wrote back. He began to look pale and sad in those days, and he was often in the village pub, drinking and talking to the people there. Then he got a job selling tickets on the railways, and left home.

The girls had an idea. I remember the day when they told me about it. Charlotte and Anne were at home on holiday, and we were all in the sitting-room after dinner one evening. Anne was playing the piano, and singing quietly to herself. She was the prettiest of the three girls, I suppose. She had long wavy brown hair, and a gentle, kind face. Emily sat on the floor beside her, stroking the ears of her dog, Keeper. Charlotte sat opposite me on the sofa, like a little child with a serious, thoughtful face. She was the smallest; her feet were no bigger than my hands.

She looked at me carefully. 'Papa,' she said. 'We want to start a school.'

'Really, my dear? Where?'

The Black Bull at Haworth
'Branwell was often in the village pub, drinking.'

'Here.'

'But Charlotte, my dear, we have no room. This house is full already.'

'Oh, but we could change the house, papa. We could build a schoolroom.'

'Well, yes, I suppose so,' I said. 'But – why do you want to do this? Isn't it better to work as governesses, in some big fine house?'

'Oh *no*, papa!' All three girls spoke at once. Anne had stopped playing, and Emily looked very angry and frightening. I could see they had thought hard about this.

Charlotte said: 'The life of a governess is terrible, papa! A governess has no time of her own, no friends, no one to talk to, and if she gets angry with the children, they just run to their mother. I couldn't *possibly* be a governess all my life!'

'It's true, papa,' Anne said. 'It's an awful life. We're so lonely away from each other. Why can't we have a school, and all live here? Then we can take care of you and Aunt Branwell when you get old.'

I looked at Emily. Her eyes were shining; I could see that the idea was important to her too.

'But why will people send their children here?' I asked. 'Haworth is not a big town, or a beautiful place. How will you find children to teach?'

'We have thought of that too, papa,' Charlotte said. 'We must learn more, and become better teachers. I have spoken to Aunt Branwell, and she will give us the money, if you agree. Emily and I want to go to Belgium, to learn French. If we can speak French well, then parents will send their children to us to learn that.'

'*Emily* will go?' I said. I looked at her. Emily had only been away from home twice, and each time she had been very unhappy. But now she looked excited.

'Yes, papa,' she said. 'I will go. Charlotte is right – we must do something. And this will help us to stay together.'

'And Anne?'

'I will stay as a governess with the Robinson family,' Anne said sadly. 'There's not enough money for us all to go, and ... the Robinsons are not so very bad.'

It was always like that. Anne was a gentle girl; she did not fight as hard as the others. Perhaps her life was easier because of that. I don't know.

But I thought it was a wonderful idea. I wrote to Belgium, and found them places in a school in Brussels, which was owned by a Monsieur Héger. I agreed to take the girls there, and for a month I wrote down French words in a little pocket book, to help me on the journey. Then, one afternoon in 1842, we caught the train to London.

I had not been to London for over twenty years, and my daughters had never been there. We stayed for three days, and then we took the night boat to Belgium, and arrived at a tall, fine school building in the centre of Brussels.

Héger himself was a very polite, friendly man – very kind. He did not always understand my French, but he showed me round the school, and talked a lot, very fast. I smiled, and tried to answer.

The two girls were very excited when I left them. As I came home on the boat, I thought: 'This is a good thing, a fine thing, perhaps. My daughters will start a good school, and Haworth will become famous. I hope Branwell can make a success of his life, too. Then my wife Maria will be pleased with us all.'

Monsieur Héger's school in Brussels
'The two girls were very excited when I left them.'

Monsieur Héger and Mrs Robinson

At first everything went well. Monsieur Héger wrote to me often. He was pleased with my daughters, he said; they were good pupils. But life at home in Haworth was hard. My curate died, and Aunt Branwell became very ill. Emily and Charlotte came home to see her, but she was dead before they arrived.

25

She was a good woman, Elizabeth Branwell. She kept my home for more than twenty years, and she taught my daughters everything she knew. But she never liked Haworth, I am sure of that. She said it was a cold, miserable place. I hope that God has found somewhere warm and comfortable for her now.

But how could I live without her? My eyes were now very bad, and I could not see to read. And our servant Tabby was older than I was. Anne could not help me – she was a governess for the Robinson family, and now Branwell had a job there too, teaching their young son. So Charlotte went back to Brussels alone, this time as a teacher in Monsieur Héger's school. Emily stayed at home to cook and clean for me. She did not like Brussels, she said. She was happy to do the housework, and live at home with Tabby and me.

She was a strange, quiet girl, Emily. She was the tallest of the girls, and in some ways she was as strong as a man. She loved to walk by herself on the wild lonely moors, with her dog Keeper running by her side. Sometimes I saw her there, singing or talking quietly to herself, and I thought perhaps she could see the people in her secret world of Gondal, and was talking to them. I know that she spent a lot of time writing alone in her room; and when Anne was at home, she and Emily often talked and wrote about the world of Gondal together.

There were sometimes dangerous people near Haworth, so I always had a gun in the house. Before my eyes were bad, I taught Emily to shoot – she loved that. Sometimes I used to practise shooting in the garden while she was making bread in the kitchen. I shot first, then I called Emily. She came out, cleaned her hands, picked up the gun, shot, and went back in to finish the bread. She was much better at shooting than I was.

But by 1844 my eyes were too bad for shooting. Emily cooked, cleaned the house, played the piano. And almost every day she went for long walks on the moors with her dog, Keeper.

She loved that dog, but she could be very hard with him, too. We did not let him go upstairs, but one day Tabby found him on my bed. Emily was very angry; her face was white and hard. Keeper was a big, strong dog, but she pulled him downstairs and hit him again and again until the dog was nearly blind. Then she gently washed his cuts herself. He never went upstairs again.

Emily Brontë's dog, Keeper, drawn by Emily
'Emily loved that dog …'

Charlotte was another year in Brussels. When she came home, she was quiet and sad. Sometimes she wrote long letters in French to Monsieur Héger, but no letters came from him. But this was a time of hope, too. The girls wrote advertisements for their new school, and sent them to newspapers, and to everybody they knew. It was exciting – they were good advertisements, and we waited for the first children to come.

We waited a long time, and Charlotte wrote more advertisements.

No children came.

Every day Charlotte and Emily waited for a letter from the postman, or for a parent to come to see them. Every day they became more miserable.

Anne left her job with the Robinsons and came home to Haworth. A month later Branwell also came home, for a holiday.

And then one morning, early, there was a knock on the door. Charlotte ran to open it. But it was not a parent – it was a letter for her brother Branwell. He went upstairs with it, smiling.

A few minutes later there was a terrible scream. We ran upstairs to Branwell's room. He lay on his bed, screaming, with a white face and wild dark eyes. The letter was in his hand.

'Branwell! What is it? What's the matter?' I asked.

He tore his hair with his hands. 'I'm ill,' he said. 'I'm cold – oh, what does it matter? She doesn't care ... I can't see her ... Oh, it's all finished now, finished for ever! I'll die without her!'

'Here, Branwell, drink this.' Emily brought him a cup of hot milk, but his hand was shaking and he nearly dropped it.

Charlotte put her hand on his head. 'He's hot, papa, he's

The Misses Bronte's Establishment

FOR

THE BOARD AND EDUCATION

OF A LIMITED NUMBER OF

YOUNG LADIES,

THE PARSONAGE, HAWORTH,

NEAR BRADFORD.

Terms.

	£.	s.	d.
BOARD AND EDUCATION, including Writing, Arithmetic, History, Grammar, Geography, and Needle Work, per Annum,	35	0	0
French, German, Latin each per Quarter,	1	1	0
Music, Drawing, each per Quarter,	1	1	0
Use of Piano Forte, per Quarter,	0	5	0
Washing, per Quarter,	0	15	0

Each Young Lady to be provided with One Pair of Sheets, Pillow Cases, Four Towels, a Dessert and Tea-spoon.

A Quarter's Notice, or a Quarter's Board, is required previous to the Removal of a Pupil.

'The girls wrote advertisements for their new school, and sent them to newspapers.'

burning,' she said. 'You must go to bed at once, Branwell.'

He went to bed, and he lay there, sometimes sleeping, sometimes shouting and crying. I tried to talk to him, but I couldn't understand what he said. Then, later, Anne explained.

She told us a terrible story. I was so angry! I nearly broke a chair with my hands as I listened. My son Branwell, Anne said, was in love with Mrs Robinson, the rich mother of his pupil. For months this lady had spoken kindly to Branwell, walked with him in the garden, talked to him alone in the evenings. He thought she would marry him when her husband died. And then there were other things, that Anne did not want to speak about.

The letter was from Mr Robinson. He was often ill, Anne told us, but his children knew about Branwell and their mother, and the servants knew too, I think. Perhaps Mr Robinson had learnt something from them, or perhaps that woman (I cannot call her a wife) had told him everything. Only one thing was certain – in his letter Mr Robinson had ordered Branwell never to return to his house or to speak to any of his family again.

My face was hot and my hands were shaking. I tried to talk to Branwell about it, but it was impossible.

'I love her, papa!' he shouted. 'You don't understand – how can you? You've never seen her!'

'I don't want to see her, my son,' I said. 'I understand that she is a bad, evil woman. I hope that God will punish her and . . .'

'Don't say that, papa!' he screamed. 'You are talking about the woman I love! She will call me back! I will see her again!'

'I hope you never see her again, my son,' I said. 'You must forget her. Branwell, listen to me . . .'

But he did not listen. He ran out of the house. He did not come back until the evening, and then he was drunk. He did not listen that day, or the next day, or any day. He began to drink laudanum as well. I thought he would kill himself.

So I think Charlotte was pleased that no parents came. No school could have a man like Branwell in it.

Currer, Ellis, and Acton Bell

At about this time, in 1845, I was almost blind. I had a new curate to do my work – Arthur Nicholls, a young man of twenty-eight. He came from Northern Ireland like myself. He was a good, hard worker. I spoke in the church on Sundays, but Arthur Nicholls did the rest of my work.

Branwell became worse and worse. Mr Robinson died in 1846, but Mrs Robinson didn't marry Branwell – oh no! She was a cold wicked woman. She sent my son Branwell away, and later married a rich old man. And so Branwell spent more and more time drinking, and taking laudanum, and walking alone on the moors.

When you are blind, you listen to things very carefully. I used to sit alone in my room and listen to the sounds of the wind outside the house. The wind talks and whispers and sings – it has many voices. I listened to the sounds of the clock on the stairs, and the wood in the fire, and the footsteps and voices of the girls walking round the house. They talked a lot to each

Haworth Church
*'I spoke in the church on Sundays, but Arthur Nicholls
did the rest of my work.'*

other, and sometimes I could hear what they said, even when
they were in another room.

Anne had had a poem published in a magazine, and one day
I heard a conversation between Charlotte and Emily. Charlotte
had found something that Emily had written, and was talking to
her about it.

'But they're wonderful, Emily,' Charlotte said. 'They're much
better than mine or Anne's.'

'They're not for people to read,' Emily said. 'They're part of
the Gondal story. Nobody would understand them, except me
and Anne.'

I realized that they were talking about some poems of Emily's.
I knew that Emily and Anne wrote a lot about the country of
Gondal, but I didn't know much about it. Emily kept all her
papers locked in her desk.

Charlotte was arguing with her. 'Emily, listen to me! These are fine poems. I think we should put some of them in a book, together with mine and Anne's, and try to publish it. People *should* read them!'

'No!' Emily shouted. Then her dog Keeper began to bark, and I didn't hear any more. But I think they talked about this again several times. I often heard voices arguing, and usually they never argued about their writing.

I wanted to tell them not to do it. I had published several small books myself, but I always lost money. I had to pay the publisher to print the books, and not many people bought them. It's an easy way to lose money. But I was too ill, so I said nothing.

I learnt, many years later, that they paid over £30 to have a book of poems printed, and that it sold two copies. I am not surprised that they didn't tell me about it; we had very little money in our house.

I began to feel that there was something wrong with my head, as well as my eyes. Several times the postman brought an old packet to our house, which was addressed to a man called Currer Bell. I told him that no Currer Bell lived in Haworth, and sent him away. But then, a month or two later, he came back again, with the same old packet.

In the summer of 1846 Charlotte took me to see an eye doctor in Manchester. We stayed in rooms in the town. The doctor decided to operate on my eyes, and the next morning we got up early. I was afraid. Could I hold my head still while the doctor cut into my eyes with a knife? Perhaps the pain would be too terrible. Perhaps I would move, or stand up, or . . .

Charlotte held my hand. As we left our rooms, we met a postman.

'Good morning, Miss,' he said. 'There's a packet here for Currer Bell.'

'Oh . . . thank you.' Charlotte sounded sad, but she took the packet, and put it in her room. She did not open it. Then we walked to the eye doctor's.

The pain was terrible, but it was over in fifteen minutes, and I didn't move. Afterwards, I had to lie on a bed in a dark room. We couldn't go home for a month. A nurse came sometimes, but Charlotte stayed with me all day.

I asked her once about the packet. She said: 'Oh, it's for a friend of mine, papa. It had a letter for me in it. I have posted it away again now.'

I didn't understand, but I didn't ask again. I lay quietly on my bed most of the day, and Charlotte sat in the next room writing. She wrote very fast, for many hours, and never put her pen down once. She seemed quiet, but strangely happy.

I was happy too. The doctor had helped; I could see again. It was wonderful – the colours, the shapes of everything were beautiful. When we came back to Haworth, I could see everything clearly at last – our home, the church, the graveyard, the moors, the faces of my Emily and Anne!

And Branwell.

Branwell's face looked terrible. White, thin, with big dark eyes and untidy hair. His clothes were dirty, he smelt, his hands shook. All the time he was either shouting or crying. And always, every day, he asked me for money.

I let him sleep in my room at night, and he kept me awake for hours talking about Mrs Robinson. I remembered his paintings, his stories, his happy childish laughter. My fine, clever son had become a drunken animal.

The winter of 1846 was terribly cold. The wind blew snow around the house and over the gravestones. A lot of children died in the village. Anne was ill, Branwell was worse. We lit fires in

Branwell Brontë
'My fine, clever son had become a drunken animal.'

all the rooms, but there was ice inside the windows in the mornings. I spent most of my time with Branwell, so I didn't think very much about the girls.

And then, one afternoon, Charlotte came into my room. I was sitting here, in this same chair, beside the fire. She had a book in her hand, and that strange, happy look on her face.

'Papa,' she said. 'I've been writing a book.'

I smiled. 'Have you, my dear?' I thought she had written another little book about Angria.

'Yes, and I want you to read it.'

'Oh, I'm afraid it will hurt my eyes too much.' My eyes were much better, but the tiny writing in the Angria books was too small for me.

'Oh no,' she said. 'It's not in my handwriting; it is printed.' She held out the book in her hand.

'My dear! Think how much it will cost! You will almost certainly lose money, because no one will buy it! No one knows your name!'

'I don't think so, father. I didn't pay to get it printed, you know. The publishers paid *me*. Listen to what people say about it in these magazines.'

She sat down, and read to me from some of the most famous magazines in England. There were long articles in them, about a book called *Jane Eyre*, by Currer Bell. They were kind articles; most of the magazine writers liked the book.

'This Currer Bell, then,' I asked. 'Is it you?'

Charlotte laughed. 'Yes, papa. It's a man's name, with the same first letters: CB – Charlotte Brontë, Currer Bell.'

She gave me the book, and went out. I began to read.

I think I read for two hours, but it seemed like ten minutes. It was a wonderful, beautiful book – the story of a little girl called Jane Eyre. Her parents are dead, so she lives with an unkind aunt and her children. Then Jane goes away to a school called Lowood. This school is a terrible place, and it is very like the school at Cowan Bridge. Jane Eyre's best friend, Helen Burns, falls ill at the school, and dies. This Helen is just like my own little Maria. When I read about her death, my eyes filled with tears. But it was a beautiful book, too; I did not want to put it down.

At five o'clock I got up and went into the sitting-room. My three daughters sat there waiting for me. Their eyes were very bright. I still had tears in my eyes, but I had a big smile on my face too. I held up *Jane Eyre* in my hand, and said: 'Girls, do you know Charlotte has written a book? And it is more than good, you know – it is very, very fine indeed!'

8

The best days, and the worst days

Emily and Anne did know, of course. They had known about Charlotte's book for a long time. *Jane Eyre* was not the first book that Charlotte had sent to a publisher. Over a year

JANE EYRE.

An Autobiography.

EDITED BY

CURRER BELL.

IN THREE VOLUMES.

VOL. I.

LONDON:
SMITH, ELDER, AND CO., CORNHILL.

1847.

The title page of *Jane Eyre* by Currer Bell
'It was a beautiful book; I did not want to put it down.'

ago she had written another book, *The Professor*, and sent it to
one publisher after another. Each publisher had sent it back, in
a packet addressed to Currer Bell. And then Charlotte had sent
it, in the same old packet, to another publisher, and then
another, and got it back again.

'Why didn't you change the paper on the packet, my dear?'
I asked.

Charlotte smiled. 'I didn't think of it, papa. The worst day
was when we were in Manchester, going to the eye doctor. Do
you remember? The packet came back then. That was the day
before I started writing *Jane Eyre*.'

'Do you mean that you started writing *Jane Eyre* while I was
lying in that dark room in Manchester?'

'That's right, papa.'

'But that's only six months ago, and here is the book in my
hand!'

'Yes, papa. The book was printed a month after I sent it to
the publisher.'

'My dear! They decided very quickly that they liked it, then!'

'I think they did, papa. After all, it *is* a good book, isn't it?'

She smiled at me. I don't think I have ever seen her so happy.
She is a very small person, Charlotte, and not a beautiful woman;
but when she smiles like that, her face shines like a fine painting.
My wife, Maria, used to look like that sometimes when I first
met her.

I took her hand in mine. 'It is a very good book, my dear. I
cannot tell you how proud I am.'

She touched my hand. 'Thank you, papa. But you must not

be proud of me alone, you know. Anne and Emily —'

'Oh no, Charlotte, please!' Emily said.

But Charlotte did not stop. '. . . Anne and Emily have written books too – books just as good as mine – and their books will soon be published as well! Let me introduce you, papa. These young ladies are not your daughters – they are Acton Bell and Ellis Bell, brothers of the famous writer Currer Bell!'

Emily's face was bright red, but Anne and Charlotte started laughing. I was very surprised.

'All three of you!' I said. 'But . . . but why do you use these strange names?'

'Because people are stupid, papa,' Anne said. 'No one thinks women can write good books, so we have used men's names instead. And now they say that Currer Bell is a writer who understands women very well!' She laughed again.

'My dears, my dears!' I held out my hands to them, and kissed each of them in turn. 'I don't know what to say. I am so pleased for you all. You have made your old papa happy today.' Something in Emily's face stopped me. 'Emily? You will let me read your book, won't you?'

She thought for a moment. 'Yes, papa. Of course. But . . . it's very different from Charlotte's. I'm not sure you'll like it.'

'You yourself are very different from Charlotte, my dear, but I love you both. You must show me the book as soon as it comes – and you too, Anne.'

I read both their books that winter. They were very different. Anne's book – *Agnes Grey* – was the story of an unhappy governess. As I read it, I was sad to think how miserable Anne

had been, in a big house away from home, w
understood her. It was a good book, but it was ha
than *Jane Eyre*.

Emily's book was called *Wuthering Heights*. It was
frightening, wonderful story. There is love in it, and ı
fear, and a man called Heathcliff, who is strong and cı
the devil himself. I read it late one night when the wiı
screaming round the house, blowing snow against a
windows, and sometimes I was afraid. When I got up to ₹

The moors near Haworth, which Emily described in her book
Wuthering Heights

WUTHERING HEIGHTS

A NOVEL.

BY

ELLIS BELL.

IN THREE VOLUMES.

VOL. II.

LONDON:
THOMAS CAUTLEY NEWBY, PUBLISHER,
72, MORTIMER St., CAVENDISH Sq.

1847.

The title page of *Wuthering Heights* by Ellis Bell
'*It was a terrible, frightening, wonderful story.*'

bed, I saw Emily sitting quietly by the fire. She was stroking her big dog, Keeper, with one hand, and drawing a picture with the other.

She looked like a quiet, gentle young woman, I thought. Tall, pretty, and also . . . There was something different about her. Something very strange and very strong. There was something in her that was stronger than any of her sisters, even Charlotte. Something stronger than even me, or her brother Branwell.

Much stronger than Branwell.

All that year Branwell was very ill. He spent more and more time drinking. He slept most of the day, and was awake half of the night. His face was white, his hands shook when he tried to write. His sisters didn't tell him about their books, or show him the new ones that they were writing. They were afraid that he would be unhappy about their success, because he had wanted to be a writer himself. He made life hard for all of us.

In September 1848 he became very ill. He coughed all day and all night. He began to talk of death, and asked us to pray with him. While we stood together, praying, he began to cough again. He fell to the ground. Emily and I put our arms round him, but he couldn't get up. There was blood on his mouth, and on Emily's dress.

When he stopped coughing, it was because he had stopped breathing. My only son was dead.

We buried him in the church beside his mother and little sisters. It was a cold, rainy afternoon. There were dead wet leaves in the graveyard, and the wind blew rain into our faces. I came back into the house soon afterwards, but Emily walked for an hour or two in the rain with her dog, Keeper. When she came back into the house, her dress was wet through.

Several days later Emily became ill. Her face was hot, she couldn't eat, she kept moving round the house. It was difficult for her to breathe, and it took her a long time to climb the stairs. Charlotte felt her heart – it was beating a hundred and fifteen times a minute.

'Let me call a doctor, Emily,' Charlotte said.

But Emily refused. 'If he comes, I won't talk to him.'

'Then go to bed and rest, please. I can light a fire in your room, and bring you milk and read to you if you like. You need rest, sister!'

'I . . . do . . . not!' said Emily slowly. She had to breathe hard between each word, and her face was as white as Branwell's had been. 'My body . . . doesn't . . . matter now. I don't . . . care . . . about it. I'll live . . . as I always . . . have.'

And so, every day, she got up at seven o'clock, dressed herself, and stayed downstairs until ten at night. She ate little or nothing, and coughed for hours. Sometimes she coughed blood. She never went out of the house, but one day Charlotte brought some heather from the moors for her to look at. Emily was lying on the black sofa in the sitting-room. Her dog, Keeper, lay on the floor in front of her.

'Look, Emily,' Charlotte said. 'I've found some purple heather for you. There are still one or two flowers left on the moor.'

'Where?' Emily asked.

'Here. Look.' Charlotte held out the small, bright purple flower.

Emily turned and looked at Charlotte, but I don't think she could see the heather. Her eyes were too bad. Charlotte put it in Emily's hands, but after a moment Emily dropped it on the floor.

At last she said: 'Charlotte, I . . . will see . . . the doctor now. If he . . . comes.' Then she closed her eyes.

Emily was so thin, and her white skin looked like paper. I knew it was too late, but I said to Anne: 'Quick! Put on your coat and fetch him, now!'

We did not have long to wait. The doctor came, half an hour later, to tell us what we already knew. Emily, my daughter, was dead.

1848 was a year of funerals. I buried many children from the village that year. There was a lot of sadness in Haworth. As I came out of the church with the dead flowers from Emily's grave, I saw three other families walk past me. They had come to visit the graves of their own dead children.

The people understood that their children were

Emily Brontë, oil painting by Branwell
*'My daughter Emily was a strange,
quiet girl.'*

with God, but no one could explain that to Emily's dog, Keeper. He followed us to her funeral, and for weeks afterwards, he lay outside her bedroom and howled.

A room at Haworth, and the sofa on which Emily died.

Arthur Nicholls

That was not the end of my sadness. Anne, too, became ill. She could not breathe, she coughed, her face was white. But she was more sensible than Emily. She took all her medicines, and did everything the doctors said. It didn't help much. In the spring she said she wanted to go to the sea, to a warmer place. The doctors told her to wait. I thought she would die before she went.

At last, in May, Charlotte went away with her. They went to York first, where they visited a wonderful church, York Minster. 'If men can make something as beautiful as this,' Anne whispered, 'what is God's real home like?'

Charlotte told me this in a letter she sent from Scarborough, a town by the sea on the north-east coast.

'*On 26th May Anne rode a donkey on the beach,*' the letter said. '*She was very happy, papa. Afterwards we went to church and then sat and watched the sea for a long time. On the 28th she was too ill to go out. She died quietly at two o'clock in the afternoon. She will be buried in a graveyard near the sea.*'

Anne was the baby of the family, the youngest and prettiest of them all. Before she died, she wrote another book – *The Tenant of Wildfell Hall* – about a woman who left her cruel husband. She was proud of it, and so was I. She was twenty-nine years old. 'I don't want to die, papa,' she said. 'I have too many ideas in my head, too many books to write.'

Anne Brontë, painting by Charlotte
'Anne was the youngest and prettiest of them all.'

When Charlotte came home the dogs barked happily. Perhaps they thought Anne and Emily and Branwell were coming home too – I don't know. But it was only Charlotte. The smallest of all my children. Not the prettiest, not the strongest, not the strangest. God had taken all those for himself. He had left me with the one who would become the most famous. And the one who nearly had a child.

48

Charlotte wrote two more books: *Shirley*, about a strong brave woman like her sister Emily; and *Villette*, about love between a teacher and a pupil. But *Jane Eyre* was her most famous book. Everyone in England talked about it; everyone wanted to read it.

Charlotte went to London and met many famous writers. I was very pleased; I loved to hear about the people and places that she saw. But she always came back to Haworth; she didn't like to be with famous people very long. And this quiet place was her home.

In 1852, just before Christmas, a terrible thing happened. I heard some of it from my room. My curate, Arthur Nicholls, opened the door to Charlotte's sitting-room, and stood there. His face was white, and he was shaking.

'Yes, Mr Nicholls?' Charlotte said. 'Do you want to come in?'

'No, Miss Charlotte – that is, yes. I mean – I have something important to say to you.'

I heard his voice stop for a moment and then he went on. 'I have always . . . felt strongly about you, Miss Charlotte, and . . . my feelings are stronger, *much* stronger, than you know. And, well, the fact is, Miss Charlotte, that . . . I am asking you to be my wife.'

There was a long silence. I heard every word, and I felt cold and angry. Mr Nicholls was a good curate, but that was all. I paid him £100 a year to help me with my work, but he had no place in my house, or in my daughter's bed! I stood up, and opened my door.

'Mr Nicholls!'

49

Arthur Nicholls
'Mr Nicholls was a good curate, but that was all.'

He turned and looked at me. I could see Charlotte behind him.

'You will leave this house at once, Mr Nicholls. I am very, very angry! You must not speak to my daughter again – ever! Do you understand me?'

The stupid man was shaking and almost crying! I thought he was ill. He opened his mouth to speak, but no words came out. Then he turned and went out of the door.

Mr Nicholls stayed in his own house for three days. He refused to eat, the stupid man, and he sent me some angry letters. But Charlotte wrote to him, to say that she would not marry him. Then Mr Nicholls said he would leave Haworth, and go to Australia.

On his last day, in church, he had to give people bread to eat. But when he held out the bread to Charlotte, he could not do it, because he was shaking and crying so much. Afterwards, the people of Haworth gave him a gold watch. He cried about that, too.

I thought it was all finished, but I was wrong. I think he wrote to Charlotte, and she wrote back. In April of 1854, he came back to Haworth. Charlotte brought him into my room. I looked at him, but I said nothing. I was not pleased.

'Papa,' Charlotte said. 'Mr Nicholls and I have something to say to you.'

I did not like that. '*Mr Nicholls and I . . .*' It did not sound good to me.

'I am busy,' I said. 'I have a lot of work.'

Charlotte smiled. 'That's because you don't have a good curate, papa. When Mr Nicholls was here, your life was easy.'

'Perhaps,' I said. 'But he was going to Australia, I thought. Why haven't you gone, sir?'

Mr Nicholls spoke for the first time. He looked very tall and proud, I thought. 'There are two reasons, sir,' he said. 'First,

Charlotte Brontë, drawn by George Richmond
'Charlotte was the most famous of all my daughters.'

because I have decided not to go to Australia. And also . . .'

He stopped, and looked down at Charlotte. She smiled up at him, and I felt my blood run cold.

'. . . and also, because your daughter Charlotte and I would like to be married. We have come to ask you to agree.'

I don't remember what I said next. I think there were a lot of unkind words between us, and some tears. But in the end I agreed. I agreed because Charlotte wanted it, not because of Arthur Nicholls.

In June that year they were married in my church. I did not go – I could not give Charlotte away to that man. But he came back here to be my curate, and he and Charlotte lived in this house with me. He is still here now.

Perhaps he will read this. If he does, he will know that he was right, and I was wrong. Mr Nicholls was, after all, a good husband for Charlotte. I understood, after a while, that he honestly loved her, and he could make her happy. She began to smile and laugh again. Her eyes shone, she sang sometimes as she worked. Our house became a home again.

She went with him to see his family in Ireland, and travelled to the far west of that country. Mr Nicholls did most of my church work for me. Charlotte began a new book – *Emma*, she called it. And one day in December 1854 she came into my room, smiling. I could see that she was excited.

'What is it, my dear? Have you finished your book?'

'No, not yet, papa. But I have something wonderful to tell you. What do you think?'

'I don't know, my dear. If it's not your book, then . . .'

'I told Arthur yesterday. I am going to have a child.'

I did not say anything. Her hand was on the table and I put my hand on it gently. It was wonderful news. I remembered when my own wife, Maria, had told me this, and how this house had been full of the laughter of little voices, and the noise of running feet. Charlotte and I sat like that for a long time, remembering.

It did not happen. At Christmas she fell ill, and in the New Year she was worse. She felt sick all the time because of the baby, and she ate nothing. She lay in bed all day, hot and coughing. Arthur Nicholls cared for her wonderfully – I think he often stayed awake all night. But it did not help.

On 31st March 1855 the last of my six children died. It was early in the morning. Arthur Nicholls was sitting by her bed, and I was standing by the door. She was asleep with her hand in his. Her face was very thin and pale.

She opened her eyes and saw him. Then she coughed, and I saw fear in her face.

'Oh God,' she whispered. 'I am not going to die, am I? Please don't take me away from Arthur now – we have been so happy.'

Those were the last words she ever said. A little while later, I walked slowly out of the house. As I went into the graveyard, the church bell began to ring. It was ringing to tell Haworth and all the world that Charlotte Brontë was dead.

Maria

And so now I have written it. It is three o'clock in the morning. The house is very quiet and the wind has stopped. I can hear the sound of the wood burning in the fire and the clock on the stairs. Somewhere upstairs Arthur Nicholls is sleeping quietly.

I know that Charlotte's friend, Mrs Gaskell, has nearly finished her book about Charlotte. Perhaps I will show her what I have written.

Perhaps. But I don't think so. I wrote to her before, and answered her questions, and that is enough. She is a writer, she can write her own book. I will keep this book in my desk, for myself – and perhaps for Arthur Nicholls. There is no need for other people to read it. My daughter Charlotte is famous already, and when Mrs Gaskell has written about her, she will be more famous still.

Patrick Brontë
'Soon I shall be buried with my wife and children.'

55

I wish my wife Maria could read Charlotte's books – and Emily's, and Anne's. Perhaps she can. We had some fine children, didn't we, Maria?

I wonder if she can hear me. It is a fine night, now that the wind has stopped. There is a bright moon, and the sky is full of stars. I think I will go outside, and walk through the graveyard to the church, and talk to Maria there.

Haworth Church and graveyard, drawing by Mrs Gaskell, 1855, from her book *Life of Charlotte Brontë*

GLOSSARY

advertisement   a notice (e.g. in a newspaper) which tells people about jobs, things to sell, etc.

article   a piece of writing in a newspaper or magazine

artist   someone who can paint and draw pictures

bark *(v)*   to make the short sharp sound that a dog makes

Bible (the)   the holy book of the Christian church

blind   not able to see

breathe   to take air into and send it out from your nose and mouth

bury   to put a dead person in a grave

candle   a stick of wax that gives light when it burns

cart   a vehicle with two or four wheels, usually pulled by a horse

coach   a large four-wheeled vehicle, which is pulled by horses and is used for carrying passengers

cough *(v)*   to send out air from the mouth and throat in a noisy way

cruel   very unkind; bringing pain or trouble to other people

curate   a young churchman who helps a rector with his church work

curtain   a piece of cloth that hangs in front of a window

devil   a very evil person; God's enemy, Satan

donkey   an animal like a small horse, with long ears

draw (past tense **drew**)   to make pictures with a pencil

drunk/en *(adj)*   excited or confused or sick because of drinking too much alcohol

duke   a title for an important nobleman

evil   very bad

funeral a church service before a dead person is buried

God the being who made the Universe

governess a female teacher who teaches children in their own home

grave the resting-place for a dead person

gravestone a stone on a grave with the dead person's name on it

graveyard a place where dead people are buried

grow up to become an adult

heather a small plant with purple flowers, which grows on moors

howl the long loud cry that a dog makes

invent to make or think of something new

kiss *(v)* to touch someone lovingly with your lips

laudanum a kind of medicine or drug which makes people feel happy

laughter the sound made when somebody laughs

moor(s) open, rough land on hills, with no trees

oil-paint a kind of paint made by mixing colours with oil

operate to cut into somebody's body in order to mend something

paint *(v)* to make a picture with coloured paints

pale with little colour in the face

papa father; a word used mostly by children (not used today)

piano a large musical instrument with black and white keys that you press to make music

poem a piece of writing in verse

pray to speak to God

print *(v)* to make letters, etc. on paper by pressing it with a machine; to make books in this way

proud feeling pleased because someone (e.g. your child) is clever or successful

publish to prepare a book, magazine, etc. for selling

pupil a child who is learning at school or from a private teacher

rector a priest in the Church of England

servant someone who is paid to work in another person's house

shy afraid of meeting or talking to people

sofa a long comfortable seat for two or three people

stroke *(v)* to move your hand gently over something, again and again

tear *(n)* water that comes from the eye when somebody cries

tiny very, very small

toy something for a child to play with

water-colours a kind of paint made by mixing colours with water

wicked very bad; evil

Before Reading

1 **Read the story introduction on the first page of the book, and the back cover. How much do you know now about this story? Are these sentences true (T) or false (F)?**

1 The Brontë children grew up in an English city.
2 The Brontë sisters are still famous for their novels.
3 All of the children died before their father.
4 Branwell Brontë taught his sisters to write.
5 The three sisters died together in an accident.
6 The Brontë family did not have a lot of money.

2 **Can you guess what happened in the Brontës' lives? Choose one or more names to complete each sentence.**

Charlotte / Emily / Anne / Branwell / none of the Brontës

1 _____ got work teaching children.
2 _____ got a job selling tickets on the railway.
3 _____ went to London to learn to be an artist.
4 _____ enjoyed shooting.
5 _____ enjoyed music.
6 _____ had a short but happy marriage.
7 _____ travelled to Belgium.
8 _____ had children.
9 _____ began drinking and taking drugs.
10 _____ had dogs that they loved.

While Reading

Read Chapters 1 and 2. Then complete these sentences with the right names.

1 _____ was the only boy in the Brontë family.
2 The children's mother, _____, died in Haworth in 1821.
3 _____ came to help with the children, and stayed in Haworth all her life.
4 _____ came from a poor family, but worked hard to get a good job.
5 _____ and _____ went to Cowan Bridge School first, and later _____ and _____ joined them.
6 _____ brought _____ back to Haworth, but she died there, and soon her sister _____ was dead too.

Read Chapters 3 and 4, and then answer these questions.

1 What present made the children start writing stories about countries called Angria and Gondal?
2 What were the little books like?
3 What different things did the children make for their secret world?
4 How did the children spend their time?
5 How was Emily different from her sisters?
6 Why didn't Branwell stay in London or Bradford?
7 What problems did Patrick have at this time?

Before you read Chapter 5 (*Looking for work*), can you guess the answers to these questions?

1 Which of the children will leave home, and why?
2 What plan will the girls think of to earn money?
3 Who will travel to another country, and why?

Read Chapters 5 to 7. Are these sentences true (T) or false (F)? Rewrite the false ones with the correct information.

1 The children preferred being at home together to working away from home.
2 Branwell got a job driving trains.
3 Charlotte and Emily went to a school in Belgium to learn French, but Emily did not go back after her aunt's death.
4 After Aunt Branwell's death, three of the children found work as teachers.
5 Emily spent a lot of time alone, walking on the moors or writing in her room.
6 Emily was never as good at shooting as her father was.
7 The girls wrote good advertisements for their school, and many people replied to them.
8 Branwell was in love with his pupil.
9 Patrick thought Mrs Robinson was a bad, evil woman.
10 The girls made £30 from their book of poems, and it sold three hundred copies.
11 After the operation on his eyes, Patrick was still blind.
12 Charlotte's first book, called *Currer Bell*, was published in 1847.
13 Patrick thought that Charlotte's book was wonderful.

Before you read Chapters 8 to 10, can you guess the answers to these questions?

1 Who dies, and in what order?
2 Who finds success before dying?
3 Who finds happiness before dying?

Read Chapters 8 to 10. Then match these halves of sentences.

1 Patrick was very surprised to learn . . .
2 All of the books were published under men's names, . . .
3 The girls didn't tell Branwell about their success, . . .
4 Branwell drank a lot and was very ill during 1848, . . .
5 Not long afterwards, Emily became ill too, . . .
6 In the spring Charlotte took Anne to Scarborough, . . .
7 When Mr Nicholls asked to marry Charlotte, . . .
8 Although he left Haworth, saying he would go to Australia, . . .
9 Charlotte did marry him in 1854, . . .
10 and in September of that year he died.
11 Patrick was very angry, and told him to leave at once.
12 but the sea air could not help Anne, and she died there.
13 because they thought he would be unhappy about it.
14 he and Charlotte continued to write to each other.
15 but they had less than a year together before Charlotte died.
16 that Emily and Anne had also written books.
17 but she refused to see a doctor until it was too late.
18 because nobody thought that women could write good books.

After Reading

1 **Match the sentences with the people. Then use the sentences to write a short description of each person. Use pronouns (*he, she*) and linking words (*although, and, before, but, who*).**

Patrick / Charlotte / Emily / Anne / Arthur Nicholls / Branwell

1 _____ was a strange, quiet girl.
2 _____ was the father of six children.
3 _____ was the most famous of the Brontë children.
4 _____ was the youngest and prettiest of the children.
5 _____ worked as a curate for Patrick Brontë.
6 _____ was the only boy in the Brontë family.
7 _____ was the only one of them who nearly had a child.
8 _____ lived longer than all of them.
9 _____ loved walking on the moors with her dog, Keeper.
10 _____ wrote only two novels.
11 _____ married Charlotte in the end.
12 _____ died before the baby was born.
13 _____ had a great talent for painting.
14 _____ was a kind, loving husband to her.
15 _____ described this wild place in her only novel.
16 _____ was very proud of his daughters and their novels.
17 _____ died in 1849, at the age of twenty-nine.
18 _____ drank a lot, became ill, and died young.

2 Imagine that Maria *did* write to her father to tell him about the school at Cowan Bridge. Complete her letter (use as many words as you like).

Dear father,

I hope that everyone is well at Haworth. The other girls here are very nice, and I _____. I am working hard at my lessons, and so are my sisters, but we _____. The teachers _____. We are often hungry, because _____. At night we _____ because _____. In the mornings we _____, and on Sundays _____. I am worried about my sisters, because _____. I don't feel very well myself, and I _____.

I want very much to _____ and make you proud of me. I am trying to be brave, but I _____. Please _____.

Your loving daughter, Maria

3 In each group of words below, there is one word which does not belong. Which is it? Then choose the best heading for each group from this list.

art / the church / illness / the moors / teaching / writing

1 _____: blood, cough, drunk, medicine, pain
2 _____: graveyard, heather, hilltop, snow, wind
3 _____: article, candle, letter, novel, poem
4 _____: Bible, curate, pray, rector, servant
5 _____: governess, lesson, pupil, schoolroom, toy
6 _____: artist, draw, famous, paint, water-colours

4 Here are nine extracts from letters mentioned in the story. Who wrote each one, and to whom? Who or what were they writing about? Then put the letters in the order that they appear in the story.

1 'Every day I hope that there will be a letter from Belgium, but nothing comes. Last year was so happy, but now I feel sad and lonely. Why don't you answer my letters? . . .'

2 'I now know everything. I have to tell you that you are no longer welcome in my house. Do not try to return here or to speak to any of my family or my servants . . .'

3 'I am making plans for Australia, but your letters give me hope. *My* feelings for *you* are as strong as ever. One word from you, and I will return at once to Haworth . . .'

4 'Thank you for answering all my questions about dear Charlotte. How I wish she was still alive to answer them herself! My book will soon be finished, I hope . . .'

5 'I'm sure you will be pleased to know that your daughters are doing very well here. They are both working hard, and your eldest daughter speaks French quite well now . . .'

6 'Please don't be too unhappy. Her last days were happy ones; she loved seeing York Minster. Think of her sitting quietly by the sea, smiling in the sun . . .'

7 'I know that you feel angry and upset, but please try to understand. My answer cannot change. If I say yes to you, Papa will be so unhappy, and I cannot do that to him . . .'

8 'Two of my daughters, aged 26 and 23, both wish to learn French. Perhaps you would be kind enough to send me some information about your school. How many pupils do you have? . . .'

9 'I am very pleased to tell you that we would like to publish your book as soon as possible. It is a very fine piece of writing, and we are sure that the name Currer Bell will soon be a famous one . . .'

5 **Which Brontë sister wrote which book? Six of the books are described below. Which books are they describing?**

_____: *Agnes Grey*   _____: *The Tenant of Wildfell Hall*
_____: *Jane Eyre*   _____: *Villette*
_____: *The Professor*   _____: *Wuthering Heights*
_____: *Shirley*

1 A story about a woman who left her cruel husband.
2 A story about an unhappy governess who is the daughter of a rector.
3 A story about a girl who lives with an unkind aunt, and then goes away to a school called Lowood.
4 A story about a strong, brave woman (a character who is in many ways like Emily Brontë).
5 A story about love and hate, and a man called Heathcliff, who is strong and cruel like the devil.
6 A story about love between a teacher and a pupil in a school in Brussels.

ABOUT THE AUTHOR

Tim Vicary is an experienced teacher and writer, and has written several stories for the Oxford Bookworms Library. Most of these are in the Thriller & Adventure series, including *Chemical Secret* (at Stage 3), or in the True Stories series, such as *Grace Darling* (at Stage 2), which is about a girl who became a famous heroine, rescuing people from a shipwreck off the north-east coast of England. He has also published two long novels, *The Blood upon the Rose* and *Cat and Mouse*.

Tim Vicary has two children, and keeps dogs, cats, and horses. He lives and works near York, which is not far from the village of Haworth, where the Brontës lived. He often visits Haworth, to take his students to the Brontë Parsonage Museum. Many of the photographs in this book are from the Museum. On the front cover of the book is the famous painting by Branwell of his three sisters, Charlotte, Emily, and Anne. You can see the place in the middle of the painting where Branwell had painted a portrait of himself, and then later painted it out. No one is sure why he did this.

OXFORD BOOKWORMS LIBRARY

Classics • Crime & Mystery • Factfiles • Fantasy & Horror
Human Interest • Playscripts • Thriller & Adventure
True Stories • World Stories

The OXFORD BOOKWORMS LIBRARY provides enjoyable reading in English, with a wide range of classic and modern fiction, non-fiction, and plays. It includes original and adapted texts in seven carefully graded language stages, which take learners from beginner to advanced level. An overview is given on the next pages.

All Stage 1 titles are available as audio recordings, as well as over eighty other titles from Starter to Stage 6. All Starters and many titles at Stages 1 to 4 are specially recommended for younger learners. Every Bookworm is illustrated, and Starters and Factfiles have full-colour illustrations.

The OXFORD BOOKWORMS LIBRARY also offers extensive support. Each book contains an introduction to the story, notes about the author, a glossary, and activities. Additional resources include tests and worksheets, and answers for these and for the activities in the books. There is advice on running a class library, using audio recordings, and the many ways of using Oxford Bookworms in reading programmes. Resource materials are available on the website <www.oup.com/elt/bookworms>.

The *Oxford Bookworms Collection* is a series for advanced learners. It consists of volumes of short stories by well-known authors, both classic and modern. Texts are not abridged or adapted in any way, but carefully selected to be accessible to the advanced student.

You can find details and a full list of titles in the *Oxford Bookworms Library Catalogue* and *Oxford English Language Teaching Catalogues*, and on the website <www.oup.com/elt/bookworms>.

THE OXFORD BOOKWORMS LIBRARY
GRADING AND SAMPLE EXTRACTS

STARTER • 250 HEADWORDS
present simple – present continuous – imperative –
can/cannot, must – *going to* (future) – simple gerunds …

Her phone is ringing – but where is it?

Sally gets out of bed and looks in her bag. No phone. She looks under the bed. No phone. Then she looks behind the door. There is her phone. Sally picks up her phone and answers it. *Sally's Phone*

STAGE 1 • 400 HEADWORDS
… past simple – coordination with *and, but, or* –
subordination with *before, after, when, because, so* …

I knew him in Persia. He was a famous builder and I worked with him there. For a time I was his friend, but not for long. When he came to Paris, I came after him – I wanted to watch him. He was a very clever, very dangerous man. *The Phantom of the Opera*

STAGE 2 • 700 HEADWORDS
… present perfect – *will* (future) – *(don't) have to, must not, could* –
comparison of adjectives – simple *if* clauses – past continuous –
tag questions – *ask/tell* + infinitive …

While I was writing these words in my diary, I decided what to do. I must try to escape. I shall try to get down the wall outside. The window is high above the ground, but I have to try. I shall take some of the gold with me – if I escape, perhaps it will be helpful later. *Dracula*

... should, may – present perfect continuous – *used to* – past perfect –
causative – relative clauses – indirect statements ...

Of course, it was most important that no one should see
Colin, Mary, or Dickon entering the secret garden. So Colin
gave orders to the gardeners that they must all keep away
from that part of the garden in future. *The Secret Garden*

... past perfect continuous – passive (simple forms) –
would conditional clauses – indirect questions –
relatives with *where/when* – gerunds after prepositions/phrases ...

I was glad. Now Hyde could not show his face to the world
again. If he did, every honest man in London would be proud
to report him to the police. *Dr Jekyll and Mr Hyde*

... future continuous – future perfect –
passive (modals, continuous forms) –
would have conditional clauses – modals + perfect infinitive ...

If he had spoken Estella's name, I would have hit him. I was so
angry with him, and so depressed about my future, that I could
not eat the breakfast. Instead I went straight to the old house.
Great Expectations

... passive (infinitives, gerunds) – advanced modal meanings –
clauses of concession, condition

When I stepped up to the piano, I was confident. It was as if I
knew that the prodigy side of me really did exist. And when I
started to play, I was so caught up in how lovely I looked that
I didn't worry how I would sound. *The Joy Luck Club*

Rabbit-Proof Fence

DORIS PILKINGTON GARIMARA

Retold by Jennifer Bassett

Fourteen-year-old Molly and her cousins Daisy and Gracie were mixed-race Aborigines. In 1931 they were taken away from their families and sent to a camp to be trained as good 'white' Australians. They were told to forget their mothers, their language, their home.

But Molly would not forget. She and her cousins escaped and walked back to Jigalong, 1600 kilometres away, following the rabbit-proof fence north across Western Australia to their desert home.

Rabbit-Proof Fence is the true story of that walk, told by Molly's daughter, Doris. It is also a prize-winning film.

The Secret Garden

FRANCES HODGSON BURNETT

Retold by Clare West

Little Mary Lennox is a bad-tempered, disagreeable child. When her parents die in India, she is sent back to England to live with her uncle in a big, lonely, old house.

There is nothing to do all day except walk in the gardens – and watch the robin flying over the high walls of the secret garden . . . which has been locked for ten years. And no one has the key.